WORKCATIONS

LASER FOCUSED GETAWAYS FOR MASSIVE
PRODUCTIVITY (DO MORE IN LESS TIME TO
ACHIEVE YOUR GOALS AND ENJOY LIFE)

HOLLY E. WORTON

Workcation Weekends:
Get More Done In Less Time So You Can Achieve Your Goals and Get the Most Out of Life

by Holly E Worton

A CIP catalogue record for this book is available from the British Library

ISBN 978-1-911161-72-1

Published by Tribal Publishing Ltd
Kemp House, 152
160 City Road
London EC1V 2NX

Please direct permissions requests to:
permissions@tribal-publishing.com

CONTENTS

Introduction   v

1. Why They Work   1
2. When to Go   5
3. Where to Go   11
4. What to Do   19
5. The Ritual   25
6. How to Stay Focused   31
7. Troubleshooting   39
8. Can't I Just Do It at Home?   45
9. Objections   51
10. Plan Your Own Workcation   55
11. Get In Touch   59
12. My Workcation Projects   61
    Appendix I   63
    Appendix II   67
    Business Beliefs   69

About the Author   79
Also by Holly E. Worton   83
Review Team   85
Holly's Grove   87
A Request   89

INTRODUCTION

"Productivity is never an accident. It is always the result of a commitment to excellence, intelligent planning, and focused effort."

— Paul J. Meyer

My workcation weekends got their start back in November 2015 when I was in Cardiff, Wales, for a workshop. It was a long drive to get there, and I arrived a day before the course began, so I could settle in and be rested for an early start the following day. I set up my computer on the desk in my room and decided to get some work done.

I soon entered hyperfocus mode and, a few hours later, realized that I had finished an incredible amount of work. There wasn't a particular project I was working on; it was just emails and regular to-do list kinds of tasks. I buzzed through my inbox, cleared out most of the emails, and made so much progress that I decided to book a hotel to work on a specific project the following month.

It wasn't clear to me what had happened, but there seemed

to be something magical about working from a hotel several hours from home. For my first workcation weekend, I reserved a room in a hotel from the same chain, located about halfway between my town and Cardiff. I suspected there was something significant about getting out of the area where I lived, but I didn't want another three-hour drive to get there.

The following month, I headed off to a hotel just before the end of the year holidays and completed an entire online program in one weekend: I recorded videos, created worksheets, and built a whole members website to host it all. I was on fire. I had embarked on my first workcation with a very ambitious project to complete, and I achieved my goal.

Almost every month since then (with the notable exceptions of the 2020-2021 lockdowns due to COVID-19), I've gone on a workcation weekend, each time to complete a specific project. It's been amazing. I'm able to hyperfocus on the selected task and get things done in record time.

What's interesting is that, more than five years later, my workcations are just as powerful as they were back in 2015. I've tweaked the details over the years to improve the experience, but my monthly workcation weekends are *the* solution to getting things done in less time.

If you have ambitious goals for your business and life, this is the solution you've been looking for to help you get things done. It will help you with completing business projects, creative projects, and more.

It's how I wrote 12 books in 12 months in 2020, despite not being able to do a workcation every single month (I doubled up and did two each month as soon as we got out of lockdown). It's how I once rebranded my business and redesigned my entire website over three days. And it's how I created a whole online course—plus website—in two days.

Before you start to question the quality of work produced in such a short time, I'd like to assure you of this: the quality of work I create during a workcation is every bit as good—if not better—than what I would working from my home office, taking longer to complete a project.

What is the workcation?

A workcation is a two-day (or longer) retreat that you can use to complete projects and get things done. It can be a business retreat, a creative retreat, or you can use it for anything else. When I use a workcation to focus on writing one of my books, I often call it a "bookcation." But it's the same thing.

It can take place on an actual Saturday-Sunday weekend, or you can plan to have it during the week. Whatever works for you. Later in this book, we'll talk about how to find the best days of the week for you.

It requires getting out of your regular workspace and going somewhere different, usually a hotel, a rental property, or an Airbnb. It needs to be a place where you have peace and quiet—where you won't be interrupted. And it needs to be some-where that doesn't offer distractions, like great nearby restau-rants or local attractions.

The workcation is about hyperfocus and getting things done—alone. It's not a couples' vacation. It's not a family getaway. If other people accompany you on your workcation, they will only serve as a distraction.

I once had a friend ask me to let her know when I was plan-ning my next workcations so that she could do the same at the same hotel. She assured me that we didn't even need to meet up while we were there; she just thought she would find it productive to do her work in her room while I was on my workcation.

But I knew that wouldn't work for me. The awareness that someone I knew was in the same hotel would be a distraction. So I kept my workcation dates a secret.

You can adapt this workcation formula to whatever works for you, and I'll show you how to do that in this book. I once did a three-day workcation to build a new website but was so burned out at the end of it that I didn't repeat the three-day workcation until last year, in 2020. Find a ritual that works for *you* and stick to it, adjusting if needed.

What the workcation is *not*

The workcation is not about combining your family holiday with remote work. That's how some people define a workcation. While that may work for some, I prefer to do one thing at a time and to do it well. As my spiritual teacher used to say, "Half a doctor is a danger to health, and half a priest is a danger to the soul."

If you're half-working and half-relaxing on holiday, you're not doing either of those things very well. When you're working, you're doing it in a beautiful location, with a plethora of distractions outside your door. And when you're relaxing or playing, you're doing it with the knowledge that maybe you should be getting some work done instead.

If this type of half-vacation, half-work retreat works for you, great. Keep it up. But this book is about a very different kind of workcation.

Why take a workcation?

I find that when I'm away from home, outside my typical work environment, I get things done more quickly and easily than I do when I'm in my home office. By booking a hotel or Airbnb and setting up a temporary workspace in a clean, clear, uncluttered environment that's devoid of my personal objects and distractions, it's easy to focus and get more things accomplished.

You may find that a workcation allows you to focus on a big project, complete a specific task such as cleaning out your inbox, or work through your to-do list more quickly and efficiently than you might in your usual workspace. In this book, we'll talk more about the types of projects you can complete on a workcation weekend.

Who this is for

This guide is for anyone who wants to increase productivity and get projects completed in record time. The workcation weekend is my top productivity tip for getting things done, and it's how I managed to write and release six books in 2016 and twelve books in 2020. I've intentionally kept this one short and to the point, including everything you need to create your own workcation weekend and avoid unnecessary time-wasting fluff.

In this guide, I will explain why workcation weekends are so powerful as a tool for getting things done (particularly creative projects). I'm going to help you understand how to create the perfect workcation for you: when to go (and when *not* to go), where to go (and where *not* to go), what to do (and what *not* to do). I'm going to share my special rituals for creating a sacred space for creative work, and I'll teach you how you can create your own rituals.

I'll help you learn how to stay focused and how to troubleshoot when things go wrong. I'll teach you how to resolve any objections from friends, family, business partners, or yourself. Finally, I'll encourage you to plan your very own workcation weekend.

Ready? Let's get started.

1

WHY THEY WORK

"Simplicity boils down to two steps: Identify the essential. Eliminate the rest."

— Leo Babauta

Workcations are effective for the same reason that people can get such great results from going to a coffeeshop to get things done. People often cite increased productivity when they spend an afternoon working from a local coffee shop. The workcation gives you the same effect, but it's a more intense experience—you're there for longer, to focus on a particular project.

Fresh environment

Your workcation will take you out of your typical workspace, whether that's your home office or workplace, and into a fresh environment. It will provide a massive change in scenery (don't try to recreate your usual workspace within your workcation space—you want it to be different). This new and different workspace can be very stimulating to your creative juices, even when it's a place you return to month after month. It can inspire new levels of focus and creativity.

Special place

This workcation place is a special place for special projects. It's a place for intensive focus and creative work. Once you've done a couple of workcation weekends, your mind will subconsciously associate this type of focused, intense work with this specific location. That's why I encourage people to find one place to go and stick with it: the workcation helps you to set the intention for intensive work. It's a time and place outside your usual office environment.

There is a term in NLP (neuro-linguistic programming) called "anchoring." It's the process by which you apply a gesture, touch, or sound when you're experiencing the peak sensation of a mental or emotional state. This state can then be re-activated by reapplying the gesture, touch, or sound when you want to experience this particular emotion or state of mind in the future.

Returning over and over again to the same location for your workcation weekends creates a similar process. Your mind will associate this place with intense creative work, and you will be able to get into this state of mind more quickly and easily. The workcation workspace isn't the exact same thing as an NLP anchor, but it's a similar concept.

That's why it's also essential to use this workcation space *only* for workcation weekends. Don't return there with your partner for a romantic weekend—find somewhere new for that. Your workcation hotel or cottage is *only* for workcation weekends.

Fewer distractions

Workcations get such great results because you remove the usual distractions of your typical workspace. You turn off all notifications and incoming communication, and you focus on just *one* thing: your workcation project.

No email, no phone calls, no interruptions from family or co-workers. Just you and your work.

Dedication to one thing

In a typical workday, you probably do many things. You may respond to emails, speak with potential clients, write a blog post, be interviewed on a podcast, and all kinds of other things. Hopefully, if you're smart and organized, you're batching your tasks into time blocks where you do the same type of activities together: you attend to your inbox for an hour, for example, rather than sporadically dipping in and out of it.

But on the workcation, you're not there to do a bunch of things. You're not there to do your usual workflow. You're there to work on *one* project (this could be something creative or something practical, as you'll learn in an upcoming chapter).

This dedication to a specific project is crucial: it lends profound importance to this work and helps you focus.

2

WHEN TO GO

"You don't have to be great to start, but you do have to start to be great."

— ZIG ZIGLAR

When should you go on your workcation weekend? Find what works for you: I like weekends because they're usually easy to book in the calendar. There was one year where I had all my workcation weekends blocked out in my Google calendar automatically, every four weeks. But then my life started filling up with lots of weekend workshops and courses, and it became harder to fit my workcations into a regular monthly slot.

Plan your year

At that point, I began to plan all my workcations at the end of each year for the following twelve months. This is how I still do it today. I go through my online calendar and block out all courses, workshops, and other events, so I know which weekends are free and which are filled with other activities.

Then, I print out an annual calendar, with all 12 months on one page, and mark it up so I can have my activities for the entire year at a glance. I use different colored highlighters to mark out the weekends occupied with other activities, and I also block out holidays and other weekday events that take up several days.

Once I have my year at a glance, I start adding my workcation weekends. I highlight them on my one-page calendar, and then I transfer them to my online calendar. I make sure not to book a workcation right after a significant event, like hiking a long-distance trail. When I walk 100 miles in a week, I'm usually physically exhausted by the end of it, and while my mind is fresh because I haven't been working for a week, it's still not a great time to do a workcation.

If things come up during the year, I drag and drop my workcations to other available dates. If I don't have enough weekends free to do one workcation each month, I'll schedule a workcation "weekend" during the week. Then I'll adjust the rest of my work around it. I make my monthly workcations a priority.

Plan for rest

I used to block out the Friday before my workcation and the Monday afterward. I would go on a long walk on Friday to clear my mind and get ready to hyperfocus on my workcation project, and I would use the Monday to rest my mind, relax, and recover from the intense weekend of work.

This system functioned well, but at some point, I forgot all about this routine, and I started forgetting about these buffer days. I began the habit of toiling away right up to the workcation, then completing a typical day in the office after I returned.

This way of doing things is not optimal because it means that I don't go into a workcation fully rested, and I don't come back from it ready to put my whole energy into my typical workday. As a result, I tend to work half-days on the Monday after a workcation. I get the most important tasks done, and I give myself permission to take it easy for the rest of the day.

If you have the freedom and flexibility to reorganize your work week around your workcation weekend, I suggest you do something special on the Friday and Monday that bookend your workcation. I'll give you suggestions on what to do later in this book.

I recommend taking some breaks before and after the workcation; I believe that this maximizes my results. Think about it this way: assuming you work a regular Monday-Friday week, you aren't taking any extra time off. You're just shifting your typical days off from Saturday and Sunday to Monday and Friday.

Plan for your cycle

I apologize if what I'm about to say is Too Much Information; I've got to share this because it's essential: whenever possible, I plan my workcation weekends around my menstrual cycle. Week 2, or pre-ovulation, is my "get shit done" mode, and my brain is incredibly fine-tuned for hyperfocus during this time.

My workcation is generally a weekend that falls in the middle of Week 2 or at the end of it, but never the weekend *before* Week 2. My brain is often not great at focusing during Week 1 of my cycle, and I find it extremely difficult to work on a major project at this time. I don't want to risk wasting a workcation weekend when my brain isn't in optimal focus mode.

If you're a woman, you may find that Week 3 works better for you. This week is typically the "I can do anything" part of your cycle and is said to be an excellent time for creating projects, as that's when we're at our most creative and productive. Sometimes my workcations will fall around Week 3, and I find that it works just as well.

If you're a woman, and you have no idea what I'm talking about, then you need to read Lisa Lister's book *Code Red: Know Your Flow, Unlock Your Superpowers, and Create a Bloody Amazing Life. Period.* In it, you'll learn about the natural "superpowers" that women have during each week of our cycle. It's a quick, fun read that was life-changing for me. I highly recommend it.

If you're a man, go ahead and plan your workcation for any week of the month. If you notice that a particular week works better for you, perhaps because the bulk of your regular work falls around a specific time of the month, then stick with that.

How many days

My workcation weekends started as a two-day event: I would arrange early check-in to my hotel at around noon on Saturday, and I would arrange a late check-out on Sunday, between 2 pm and 4 pm. While I split my workcation over two days, I was generally at the hotel for just over 24 hours.

Sometimes, I would go down to the hotel's bar after check-out and enjoy a coffee while finishing my project. This small extension was a great way to extend my workcation. And since I was already in hyperfocus mode, I was able to take advantage of the extra couple of hours and get things wrapped up with my project.

The first time I attempted a three-day workcation was when I rebranded my business and redesigned my entire website. It was exhausting, and I felt burned out. I resolved never again to do a three-day workcation.

But then COVID-19 happened in 2020, and all accommodation was closed. When things re-opened, I wasn't that crazy about the idea of going to a huge hotel like I used to. I started looking into smaller properties on Airbnb and Flipkey (a Trip-Advisor website).

Because these smaller properties didn't allow me the flexibility of a large hotel in terms of early check-in and late check-out, I started planning three-day workcations. After some trial and error, I've found the perfect place (more on that in the next chapter). I check in as early as possible, and I arrange a late check-out if I can. Most properties are willing to be flexible with the check-out time if they don't have anyone checking in the same day, and their cleaner won't be coming in until late on the day of your check-out or until the following day.

Weekday or weekend

You might find that Saturday and Sunday are perfect for your workcation. Or you may prefer to book your workcation during the week. Play around with it and see what gets you the best results.

The days you choose may also determine where you stay (more on that in the next chapter). Big hotels that specialize in conferences are often more expensive during the week and cheaper on the weekends. Smaller properties popular with couples seeking a weekend getaway will probably be more costly on the weekend, less so during the week.

If money is an issue, plan your workcation around where you're going to stay and when. However, remember that you may be able to include the meals and accommodation as a business expense—check with your accountant, who will know if you this is possible.

Do what works for you

Try a weekend, then try two weekdays. See what works for you. What gets you the best results?

The same goes for the length of your workcation: start with two days, and evaluate how it went. Then try three-days, and see what you think. You can also adjust the length of your workcations depending on the size of each project you're working on.

3

WHERE TO GO

"I don't wait for moods. You accomplish nothing if you do that. Your mind must know it has got to get down to work."

— PEARL S. BUCK

At first, I thought that the magic of getting things done so efficiently happened because I was in Cardiff, a three-hour drive from where I live. That's why I booked my first workcation in Swindon, which I thought would be sufficiently far from home. However, the drive was long and tedious, and I got stuck in traffic because it was just before the Christmas holidays. That led to my decision to plan my next workcation a bit closer to home.

My subsequent workcations were in Basingstoke and Farnborough, both located just an hour from where I live. This journey was a much more leisurely drive for my workcations, and I still felt like I was outside my usual environment. Plus, much of the trip was quite pretty. These new locations worked for some time.

Eventually, I moved even closer to home: to the Crowne

Plaza in Crawley, near Gatwick Airport, only 25 minutes away. The Crowne Plaza was perfect for a few years: it was far enough away that I felt like I was outside my typical surroundings (I never go to Crawley for anything but workcations), and the drive to get there is down pretty country roads. This lovely drive made for an excellent, stress-free beginning and end to my workcation.

These places (Swindon, Basingstoke, Farnborough, and Crawley) are also devoid of distractions. They're certainly not tourist towns, and there are no local tourist attractions I could think of visiting there outside of my workcation. They're all perfectly fine places to go, but my point is that I never had to worry about an enticing beach or riverside path or lakeside trail to distract me from my work.

When I began staying at properties on Airbnb and Flipkey, I tried a couple of different properties before finding the perfect one. The first place I stayed at was a tiny shepherd's hut near Billingshurst, in West Sussex. It was a pretty little hut, beautifully decorated inside. It was warm on chilly days and cool in the warm weather.

It looked out onto a grassy paddock filled with sheep, and the hut was conveniently located far enough away from the main house that I never even met the owners. We communicated via text, and they left me alone to do my thing.

It was small and comfortable, with everything I needed— including a small table meant for dining, but that also made the perfect desk. The only downside was that it was right on a busy road even though it was located in the countryside. I could hear the cars passing all day long, and I could also hear the sound of trains off in the distance.

I wanted peace and quiet, which I eventually found in what has now become my favorite spot for my workcations. It's a half-hour from home, and it's a little summerhouse in the garden of an old farmhouse. The small dining table (my desk) looks out on a grassy field, and if I lean a bit to the side, I can see the beautiful garden, which is full of flowers.

The hosts don't mind if I take a stroll around their garden, which I rarely do. I'm usually too busy getting things done on my computer. But I have a gorgeous green view out the window as I do so.

Get away from home

Wherever you go, find a place that feels like you're outside your typical environment: somewhere you don't usually go for work, or networking, or shopping, or anything. The only time I have ever been to Basingstoke, Farnborough, or Crawley has been for my workcations. Going to those locations got me in the zone for a workcation because my mind knew that's what I was there for.

Be sure not to travel *too* far. You'll waste time getting to and from your workcation that would be better spent on your project, and you may get stuck in stressful traffic, which might destroy the peace of mind you need to hyperfocus on your work.

My requirements

My requirements for a workcation are as follows:

- Close to home: between 30-60 minutes
- Room service, or a small fridge to keep my food
- A kettle for tea and hot drinks (this is pretty much standard everywhere in the UK, so it's not hard to find—but I have stayed in the occasional Airbnb without a kettle in the room)
- A self-contained property that is *not* linked to the primary residence

- A desk or a table suitable for working on a computer (be sure that there's a chair that looks comfortable enough to sit in for long hours)
- A quiet location: no noisy neighbors, roads, or nearby trains

Nice-to-haves:

- Pretty drive between home and the workcation destination
- Possibility for early check-in and late check-out
- Pretty view from my desk
- If I'm staying in a large hotel, I request the quiet zone if they have one (this is usually the highest floor)
- A decent internet connection (though this isn't a necessity for me, since I have an excellent data plan on my phone, which I often use as a backup)

My recommendations for a hotel

If you want to go to a big hotel, I recommend finding one that's part of a major hotel group so that you can earn points for your stay. I'm a member of the IHG Rewards Club, and I started my workcations at Holiday Inns before eventually upgrading to the Crowne Plaza, which isn't that much more expensive, though the rooms are much better. Both hotels are part of the IHG group—which means that I accumulate points at both of them —and I get a discounted room rate and extras like early check-in and late check-out (when possible).

By collecting points in the IHG Rewards Club, I have been able to have *free* workcations every once in a while. It's such a pleasure to go into the app to book a workcation and find that I can get a free room. Most major hotel groups have some kind of loyalty program like this.

Once you find a hotel that you like, plan to go back there again and again. It will pay off. They will mark you as a repeat guest, and you may be eligible for unexpected upgrades. My first company was in the hospitality industry, and I know from first-hand experience that hotels are much more likely to upgrade a returning guest than a first-timer.

The first time I stayed at the Crowne Plaza in Gatwick, they upgraded me to a Club Room for free. I liked it so much that I always booked this upgraded room during future stays. If you're paying for a Club Room upgrade, it's about £25 extra, but it gets you free non-alcoholic drinks and snacks all day in the club lounge, complimentary buffet breakfast, and free evening drinks and canapés. Plus, the rooms are larger and more nicely furnished, which is especially nice if you'll be doing videos inside. Sometimes, an upgrade pays for itself.

Note that upgrades may also present the risk of a distraction to your project. I used to visit the Club Room to take a break in the evening and have a drink and some canapés, but then, of course, I found it hard to get back into my work once I had had a glass of wine. So I stopped visiting the Club Lounge, though I continued to book the better Club Room.

Because the Crowne Plaza is such a large hotel, it has a Quiet Area on the sixth floor. It's located up a little stairway at the end of the hallway on the fifth floor (which is relatively easy to miss) and through a door that only allows access to people staying in the Quiet Area. There are signs reminding guests to be quiet there, which means that it usually is relatively peaceful.

The Crowne Plaza view isn't great (busy roads and giant car parks), but the rooms have big windows that let in much sunlight. And there's room service, so I can order dinner without having to leave my room. There's also a mini-fridge, which means that I can bring salads and ready-made meals if I prefer.

My recommendations for a smaller property

Find a place that looks quiet. Be sure that it's a separate building and not connected to the primary residence. My husband once booked a workcation from an Airbnb that was attached to the main house. He could hear their phone ringing and their conversations through the door that linked his accommodation to their home. While the door was kept locked, the sound passed through it quite easily.

Look on a map to ensure it's not on a major road or near any train stations. I may be a stickler about noise, but I love it when the only sounds I can hear are the birds singing and the wind rustling through the trees.

Make sure the room has a good table or desk and a proper chair to sit in. While this may not be the most ergonomic of workspaces, it should have some level of comfort, even if it's a dining chair with a soft cushion on it. One gorgeous property that I stayed in last year was a French roulotte—kind of like a large shepherd's hut—, but the little table only had stools to sit upon. While the roulotte was quite spacious, there wasn't a proper chair in the place. Sadly, it won't work for that reason alone.

Once you've established that you like a place and would like to return, ask your host if you can book directly with them the next time. They will probably offer you a discount to book through them, as they won't have to pay the Airbnb or Flipkey commission. If they don't offer, then ask.

If the property serves breakfast, and you don't require a morning meal, ask if you can get a discount if you forego this. When booking directly with the hosts, you have a bit more flexibility.

To clarify things: I'm not suggesting you drive a hard bargain for the price (you want to establish a good relationship with the hosts), but be aware that you may be able to negotiate a bit if you're saving them the booking commission or the hassle of cooking you breakfast. Don't be shy—ask politely!

Once you've established a relationship with the hosts, ask about early check-in and late check-out. If the property is cleaned in the morning, you may be able to check in around noon. And if no one is checking in after you depart, the hosts might allow you to stay until late in the afternoon.

Where *not* to go

You'll want to avoid choosing a place just because it's cheap. If you can tell that the location won't be ideal, then find somewhere else. Do some more research, and see if you can find a better place at a similar price.

Don't travel too far from home. You want to be outside your usual stomping grounds, but you don't want a long commute to your workcation. It's wasted time.

You'll also want to avoid an Airbnb where you've got one room inside a residential house with a family. You'll have no privacy, and you'll probably be subjected to all the sounds of having other people in the house. The same goes for a property that shares a wall with the primary residence.

Be sure to avoid a property that doesn't have a proper workspace, even if the rest of the room is beautiful. You're there to work intensively, and you need to do it in relative comfort. A wooden stool does not make a comfortable desk chair, even if you pop a cushion on top of it.

Also, remember that rural locations present different challenges for the workcation. On one trip to the shepherd's hut, the host warned me that they would be shearing sheep in the barn next to my hut. Thankfully, it wasn't a problem—their shearing was quiet, and I barely noticed they were working there—but other types of farm work are much noisier.

If your summerhouse or cottage is located within a big garden, you might be bothered by a leaf blower or other garden devices. If noise can be a source of distraction to you, bear this in mind. Know what types of noise you find disruptive and plan in advance to avoid them.

Finally, don't go somewhere that you go for other purposes. If your family has a cabin in the woods or a second home on the beach, don't use those spaces for your workcation. Your mind associates those locations with fun, play, and family—not with work. The exception to this rule is if you already use those spaces for creative work, and you find that you quickly get quality creative projects completed there.

Do what works for you

Are you a country person or a city person? Do you prefer quiet cottages or high-rise hotels? Try different types of settings and see what works for you.

I honestly never thought I'd leave my beloved Crowne Plaza, but now that I've found my pretty little country cottage, I can't imagine going back there. The view from my workspace and the quiet atmosphere, interrupted only by birdsong, sells it for me.

4

WHAT TO DO

"If you don't pay appropriate attention to what has your attention, it will take more of your attention than it deserves."

— DAVID ALLEN

F rom what I've experienced, the key is to set *one* goal or choose *one* specific project to work on and *only* do that work on the workcation. You can use your workcation to focus on any project you've planned for your business—or a creative activity for a long-neglected hobby. If you're stuck finding a project, go through your to-do list and see what's been sitting there for a while, perhaps because you haven't had a big chunk of time yet to complete it.

Set boundaries

You need to set boundaries, and you need to uphold them. Your workcation is about the *one* thing that you chose, and only that. I usually decide on the project the week of or the day before the workcation. It must be something that feels good to be working on—if it's a project that I'm not passionate about when the workcation comes around, then I pick something else. I don't force myself to stick to a prescribed schedule of projects.

For example, every year, I plan out my publishing calendar of all the books I want to write or re-write in the new year. I map out which books I want to release each month, and I create a spreadsheet with the project and launch dates.

But when I get ready to go on my next workcation, I might pick a different book to work on than I originally planned. It all depends on what I feel like working on. If I choose something else, I shift the rest of my publishing calendar around to reflect that.

I'll talk more about my workcation ritual in the next chapter, but what's important is that I remove all distractions. I close the tab for my email inbox. I silence the notifications on my phone, tablet, and computer by putting everything in Do Not Disturb mode. I shut myself off from outside communication. And if I'm staying in a smaller property, I gently make it clear that I'm there to work or write in peace—I'm not available for chitchat.

This last bit is essential. My husband and I once rented a little studio apartment to use as an external office space for our workcations. It was a cozy little space above the garage of a residential home. This location meant that the landlords were always around, and if they saw our car in the driveway, they often popped up to say hello and make sure we were okay. But then the conversations would drag on a bit.

Our cozy little studio ended up being the worst investment ever. I was so afraid of being interrupted that I never got good work done there. I couldn't concentrate. I think that we didn't use the studio more than about five or six times within the six-month contract between the two of us. Each visit cost us much more than a single workcation—and even though we had purchased a bed so we could sleep overnight in the studio, neither of us ever slept there.

Don't make this mistake. Set boundaries, uphold them, and find a place that respects them.

Workcation projects

While I call it a *work*cation weekend, you can use it for any project—whether business, personal, or creative. These days, I mostly reserve my workcations for writing my books, which is why I often call them my "bookcation" weekends. As I said earlier, I pick and choose from my list of publishing projects which book I feel like working on when my workcation weekend comes around.

I also keep a list in Evernote of all the essential little tasks that I somehow never manage to find the time to complete. I print out the list before each workcation, and if I finish my main project early and I have time left over, I pick from my Evernote list and get things done.

Remarkably, the magic of the workcation weekend means that I often efficiently complete several of these tasks that I regularly procrastinate on when I'm working from my home office. There's something about getting outside of my typical workspace that makes it easy to get things done.

Here are some ideas for your workcations. I prefer to use mine for creative business projects (like writing), but you can use them for any big task or activity.

For example, if you don't have a bookkeeper, you may get behind on your bookkeeping. A workcation could be the solution to get caught up. If you don't have an accountant to do your taxes, you may want to take a workcation to get your taxes done.

A reminder: even though it's called a *work*cation weekend, you can use the time for personal projects. Sometimes, it merely takes getting out of our usual work and living space to see the big picture of things—and that broader perspective is enough to help us see the changes we need to make in our lives.

My point? You can use your workcation for any project that you want.

Business ideas

- Build a new website
- Rebrand your business
- Clear out your inbox
- Create an online course and a membership website to host it
- Put together a new opt-in gift for your email list
- Write a new autoresponder series for your email list
- Create a business plan or marketing plan or update your existing ones if needed
- Get some distance from your business and look at the bigger picture: adjust your goals/plans if necessary
- Plan your goals and projects for the new year or next quarter
- Get caught up on your bookkeeping
- Do your taxes

Personal ideas

- Plan your personal goals and projects for the coming year
- Look at the big picture of how your business or career fits into your life, and adjust as needed

- Get in touch with friends you've lost contact with: write long emails or letters to reconnect

Creative ideas

- Write or edit a book or part of a book
- Write a collection of poetry or songs
- Write all your blog posts for the next few weeks/months
- Record a block of podcast episodes for your podcast (if the room is appropriately soundproofed)
- Use the backdrop of your space to record videos for your YouTube channel

What *not* to do

Don't go into your workcation without a plan. You should have *one* project for your workcation, and it should be something that you're willing to commit to.

Yes, I have a list of little tasks that I've been procrastinating on, and I use those to fill in the extra time. One workcation project could be to work my way through that list. But I would have to commit to this project before going into my workcation.

In the same way, clearing out my inbox of the emails I've been procrastinating on would be another good workcation project, and it's one that I've done before. But again—it's something I would commit to as a project. I wouldn't just aimlessly dip in and out of my inbox over the course of the weekend.

You could also dedicate a workcation to creating content for your blog, podcast, or YouTube channel. If you choose this, I'd recommend picking one type of work (writing, audio, or video) and dedicating your workcation to that. Part of the power of the workcation comes from working on one type of task or activity.

You need to have the right mindset going into the workcation: you'll be focusing on an important project, and you're going to commit to this project and dedicate your time and energy to it. Part of the magic of the workcation comes from this commitment and dedication.

Do what works for you

While I highly recommend picking *one* project for your workcation, maybe that doesn't work for you. Perhaps you have a big list of things and pick and choose once you get there. If this truly works for you, go for it. But I suggest you try the "traditional" one-project workcation first, so you can get a feel for the power of focusing on just one thing.

5

THE RITUAL

"Ritual and ceremony in their due times kept the world under the sky and the stars in their courses. It was astonishing what ritual and ceremony could do."

— Sir Terry Pratchett

Earlier I called the workcation a ritual, and it is. I have a precise formula for my workcation weekends, and I do things in the same way each time. If I'm going to the Crowne Plaza, I check into the hotel at roughly the same time on Saturday, and I check out at the same time on Sunday (when possible). I bring the same foods to eat in my room and the same kinds of herbal teas to drink as I work. I order the same dinner for room service on Saturday, and I often eat the same lunch after I've checked out of my room on Sunday.

I've also had the hotel make a note in the system that I prefer the Quiet Area, and I've even asked them to make a note of the specific rooms I like. If those are available, I'll get one. If not, they'll allocate me a room somewhere else. But at least I have a better chance of getting my preferred accommodation.

While this may sound boring to you, it serves as a kind of anchor for the experience. My brain and my body know what's coming. There are no surprises. I can leave my mind to focus on the workcation project.

Not only that, but it means that I don't have to think about any of the minor details. I don't have to ponder what to eat or drink. I do the same thing I do every time, focusing all my creativity on my project.

When I stay at the little cottage, I check in and check out at roughly the same time. I bring the same foods to eat and the same teas to drink. Each time, I put my suitcase in its usual place, and I set up my desk as I always do.

Power talismans

I bring my power talismans: a pair of teal glass fairy wing earrings that I love, and some crazy gold sequined fingerless gloves that are my power gloves. I wear one or both of these to get in my power work mode. They make me feel focused and sparkly, and I wear them for many of my creative projects.

If this sounds weird and woo-woo to you, that's fine. You do you. But if you have an outfit or some shoes that make you feel powerful and creative, be sure to wear those.

Bring whatever it is that you need to get in the right mood for your workcation. If you have a favorite crystal or trinket that you'd like to have on your desk, bring that. But be wary of recreating your regular office space in the workcation space.

You want this to be a unique, *different* workplace. So be sure to wear different clothes or set up your desk in a distinct way.

Setting boundaries

If I'm going to the Crowne Plaza, I check into the hotel and go straight to my room, putting the "do not disturb" sign on the door handle outside. I don't take it off until I check out the following day.

If I'm staying at the cottage, I go straight there. The host will often stop by quickly to greet me later, but she knows that I'm there to work and is very respectful of my time. I do enjoy a quick chat with her, as I know that she recognizes that I'm there to get things done on my workcation.

Setting up my space

I take the luggage rack out from the wardrobe and set it up in a convenient location in the room, setting my suitcase on top and opening it up.

I clear off the desk and put the magazines and hotel information in a drawer where I can't see them. I take my computer out of my bag and set it up, plugging it in. I take my notebooks out and set them up alongside my laptop. I get my highlighters and pens and get them ready on the desk.

I put my food away in the minibar refrigerator (which is empty, with plenty of space for my snacks), and I set up my tea station by organizing my box of mixed herbal teas. I put my tea glass next to the teas, and I fill the kettle with water.

While the kettle boils, I adjust the air conditioning and the lighting in the room. I take off my shoes and put on my slippers. Once my tea is ready, I take it to the desk and sit down.

Gratitude and prayer

I open up my journal and write a list of ten things that I'm grateful for. I set my intention for what I want to get done on the workcation, and I ask the angels for help in getting everything completed in the best way possible. (You can ask the Universe for help, or God, or whomever you usually ask for assistance. Or you can ignore this step!)

Often, I will softly chant a few awens before getting started. Awen is the Welsh word for poetic inspiration, and it has also been described as flowing spirit. I like to think of it as divine creative energy. When I chant awens before starting my project, I'm calling the energy of spirit to guide me in my work.

If you practice prayer, this is a great time to ask for spiritual guidance.

Getting to work

I turn on my computer, connect to the wifi, and put on my reading glasses. I set my phone and iPad to Do Not Disturb mode. If clearing my inbox is not my selected project for this workcation (and it rarely is—I think I've only done that once), then I close the tab for my email.

Once all of this is done, I'm ready to get started. I work non-stop, breaking only to make a cup of herbal tea and to use the bathroom. Then it's straight back to it.

In the early days of my workcations, I would work until about 9 or 10 pm, when I would phone for room service. I would continue to work as I waited for my (very late) dinner. After I ate, I would rest and then take a bath. I would have a mug of hot chocolate and then get ready for bed, sometimes listening to a guided meditation or ASMR (calming sounds) to relax before going to sleep.

The next morning I would get up at 7 am, which for me is early (I usually wake up at 8 am). I would do my morning meditation exercises, then head downstairs for breakfast. When I returned to my room, I would phone the front desk and ask for a late check-out, which they were usually able to accommodate. This late check-out meant that I could stay in my room until 2 pm, though sometimes I managed to remain until 4 pm.

I write another gratitude list before returning to my computer to work until just before my check-out time when I would pack everything up and head downstairs to check out of my room. After that, I might go to the hotel bar and lounge area, where I would set up my computer once again while I had lunch. I usually head home around 4 pm.

Now that I go to the cottage for a three-day workcation, my days aren't as intense. I check in around noon, and I get straight to work. I now eat earlier in the day, so I will have a break around 3 pm to have a meal, and then I get back to work until around 8 or 9 pm when I stop for the day.

I listen to a guided meditation or ASMR, and then I go to bed. I find that having an hour or so of listening to something relaxing helps me separate the hyperfocus of the workcation from my sleeping time. If I don't take this time to disconnect, I spend much time tossing and turning in bed, thinking of my project and all the little details I want to work on the next day.

My second day usually starts with breakfast; then I get straight into work. I'll break for a meal around 3 pm, and then I continue in the same manner as the day before.

On my check-out day, I'll have breakfast and then work non-stop until my departure time. I take full advantage of my time on the property.

My cottage workcations are incredibly powerful, and while my working days aren't as long as they used to be when I would go to the Crowne Plaza, I spread the work out over a more extended period, and I feel less burned out when I get back home.

Do what works for you

Create your ritual for your workcations. Wear the clothes that get you in the right mood for your project. Figure out how you need to feel to complete it, and bring the necessary elements to make that happen.

Do you need to feel creative? Powerful? Strong? Unstoppable? Bring the clothes, accessories, or elements that will invoke that feeling in you.

Look at motivational images (I have a screensaver on my computer that helps me get into the right state of mind for my creative work). Bring your vision board and hang it up on the wall or prop it up on your desk. If you work with affirmations, repeat the most important affirmations that will get you feeling focused and ready for the intensive work that will follow.

If you're spiritual or religious, say a prayer. Or state your intention silently or out loud. It could be something simple as: "I intend to have a joyful and productive workcation weekend."

Clearly stating our intentions can be powerful. It clarifies our plan to ourselves and whoever is listening (the Universe, Spirit, or whatever you believe in). And it creates a mini-ritual that gives a sense of importance to the work you are about to begin.

6

HOW TO STAY FOCUSED

"When walking, walk. When eating, eat."

— ZEN PROVERB

The key to a successful workcation is remaining focused on the *one* project that you've planned to complete during your stay. Here are my top tips for staying focused and removing distractions during a workcation weekend.

Set a clear goal

Don't go on a workcation to simply do a bunch of work in a different setting. Go with *one* specific goal or project or a list of mini-projects: I've gone on a workcation to create an online program, to build an entire website, and to write my books.

While I usually choose a single project to work on during my workcation, I once completed a series of mini-projects that I *planned in advance.* Planning is essential: I didn't just go into the workcation wondering what I was going to do; I made a brief list of small projects, and I worked through them one by one.

Make it achievable

Be certain that whatever goal or project you plan for your workcation is doable: you want to make sure that you have enough time to complete your project (or finish a specific part of it), so you have a sense of fulfillment at the end. If you want to clean out your inbox, that's great—but be sure that you have enough time to do so. If you've got thousands of emails that have never been replied to or archived, that might take more than a weekend to finish.

Set yourself a reasonable goal, and work towards it. If you have a larger plan or project, break it down into a manageable, weekend-sized chunk.

For example, I can write a 15,000-word book like this one in a single workcation. Then, I can run it through Grammarly to fix basic grammatic errors before sending it to a human editor. But I can't use a single workcation to write one of my longer books, like my 81,000-word *Alone on the South Downs Way*. That may take three or four workcations.

Plan, plan, plan

Ensure that you bring everything you need to work on your project: notebooks, notes, printouts, whatever. If you've left a vital part of the project at home, then you won't be able to get things done.

I have a dedicated packing list for my workcation weekends. I print it out each time I go and highlight each item as I pack it. I'll include that list later in the book so you can personalize it for yourself.

Get enough sleep

If you can, be sure to get enough sleep the night before your workcation. When you haven't slept well, you may find it hard to get anything done. But when your mind and body are well-rested, you'll be able to hyperfocus on your workcation project.

Also, don't plan any strenuous physical activities right before you go away. If you've got a 35km run planned one week, make sure you do it well in advance of your workcation. You don't want to be tired and achy as you sit in a chair all day working on a creative project.

Use caffeine mindfully

I don't drink a lot of caffeine—just one espresso in the morning. After that, all my hot drinks are herbal teas, except for an occasional green tea with jasmine. I never drink energy drinks or soda.

I also don't want to build up a tolerance to caffeine because I prefer to save it for when I truly need it—for a long run, or to focus on a workcation project. While I don't drink endless cups of coffee during a workcation, if I feel my energy flagging, I might have a black tea or espresso.

Use food mindfully

I practice intermittent fasting. I used to do alternate day fasting —two meals every other day—but now I'm back to OMAD, or one meal a day. That's 23 hours of fasting and a single one-hour meal.

While intermittent fasting usually leads to an increased focus in those who practice it (including myself), I will often have two meals a day on my workcations: breakfast and lunch. It all depends on how I'm doing with my project: if my rumbling tummy is distracting me from my work, or I'm feeling my energy levels lowering, then I'll have a meal.

If you're the kind of person who prefers small snacks throughout the day, and you know that this helps increase your focus, then go with that. Figure out what works best for you.

Exercise if it helps

Exercise is an essential part of my life (mostly hiking, trail running, and kickboxing), but it's not a part of my workcations. While I have considered bringing my running gear for a country run on the trails around my workcation cottage, I've never actually done it. I prefer to focus on my project.

But if exercise helps you to work better, then bring what you need to go on a walk or a run (or a bike ride!) on your workcation. You might find an evening walk after you finish your work each day will help you to disconnect from your project before bedtime.

Take breaks if needed

When I'm on a workcation, my only breaks are what I call "T&P." I put on the kettle, go to the bathroom, and then make myself a fresh herbal tea when I come back. This break happens about once an hour, so it gets me up from the desk and moving around.

If you require regular breaks to keep focus, then take them. I despise the Pomodoro technique (that's short, 25-minute blocks or work time), but if it works for you, then do it. I'm capable of focusing effectively for much longer than 25 minutes, so for me, it would be a massive distraction to stop working after such a short period.

Use music if it helps

I need absolute silence for hyper-focusing on a workcation project. That's why it's so essential for me to have a quiet country cottage, where the only sounds are those of birdsong. Cars and trains annoy me when I'm in focus mode.

I also can't listen to music, even instrumental music that's designed to help with focus—or nature sounds, like the ocean or a babbling brook. The birds outside don't bother me, but birds on a recording do. I can hear a tawny owl hooting as I write this, and it sounds magical.

But many people find that certain music or sounds help them focus, so know what works for you and do that.

Meditate

If you meditate, you might want to do that at the start of your workcation days. You can meditate in silence or use a guided meditation. This can help you to relax, clear your mind, and get set for a weekend of hyperfocus.

I also like to recommend what I call my "task meditation." This particular type of "meditation" consists of quieting your mind *as if* you were about to meditate. But instead of putting aside any thoughts that arise, you write them down.

The "task meditation" is an excellent way of clearing your mind of all the little daily tasks that are cluttering it up. Maybe you forgot to buy milk. Write that down. Perhaps you need to remember to call your sister about that thing. Write that down.

You can make a list of all these little things, and put it aside for when you return from your workcation. Once you're back in your office, you can put them into your to-do list and get them done. This "task meditation" is *not* designed to create new things for you to do during your workcation—it's designed to clear your mind of any distractions.

Prioritize your project

Work on the *one* project that you've planned for—and nothing else. Stay on track. If you find your mind wandering or your fingers typing "facebook.com" into your browser, stop and return to your project.

Remind yourself that you have invested money in accommodation to get this particular project completed. This is not an office away from home. This is a special place for special projects.

The more you train yourself to focus on this one task, the easier it will be to do so in the future.

Minimize distractions

Don't allow yourself to get distracted. If you're working on a book and find yourself opening up your Gmail tab to see if anything has popped in, stop yourself and close it.

If you're waiting for a particular email to come in that you need to urgently reply to, see if your business partner can access your email for you at regular intervals and notify you that it's arrived. However, I highly recommend planning your workcation around times when your business partner or staff won't urgently need you in your business. I know this isn't always possible, but try to make it happen.

And ask yourself: just how urgent is this? Can it wait until Monday? Most things can.

If you don't need wifi for research, then don't connect to the hotel's wifi. Keep your phone and tablet hidden, away from view, if you think they might distract you. Put them in Do Not Disturb or Airplane Mode.

Know what your typical distractions are, and plan ways to avoid them. Use plugins for your browser that will block certain websites from you.

If other guests in the hotel are noisy, or if you're on a low floor and are bothered by street noise, put your earbuds in and listen to music or nature sounds. I always bring earbuds on a workcation—just in case. I prefer to work in silence, but they're a must-have in case of emergency (you'll want to block out any distracting sounds like leaf blowers, children crying, or traffic).

Set a deadline

Know what time you want to stop working on the first day and when you plan to finish the second day. Calculate how much work you can get done in those periods. That will help you plan the work that needs to get done, and it will encourage you stay on track.

Do what works for you

The more workcations you do, the better you'll plan them around the right schedule for you. I was shocked to read through my writings about my early workcations when I wouldn't have dinner until 9 or 10 at night and then go to bed around 1 am. My schedule has changed quite a bit since then!

On your workcations, go to bed whenever it's best for you, even if that's wildly different from your usual bedtime. Wake up extra early or a bit late. Find your unique workcation schedule that may differ from your regular workday schedule.

My usual workday is from 11 am to 7 pm. But on workcations I usually find myself working from 8 am to 8 pm—sometimes even later.

7
_____

TROUBLESHOOTING

"With every experience, you alone are painting your own canvas, thought by thought, choice by choice."

— OPRAH WINFREY

S ometimes we have the best of intentions and the best of plans, and things still don't go as expected. What to do if your workcation feels like a flop? You troubleshoot.

The question you need to ask yourself is: what's wrong? What's not working?

Can't focus

If you can't focus, figure out what the exact problem is. Any environmental distractions (like loud neighbors or a noisy street) are easy to fix. Pop in your earbuds.

Are you tired? Hungry? Thirsty? Those problems are also easy to fix. Have a nap, a snack, or a drink. Then get back to your project.

Maybe you need a break. While I love working for hours on end, with only an hourly T&P break, that might not be ideal for you. Perhaps you like the Pomodoro technique. Take a break—maybe get off the computer and go for a walk—and see if that helps.

Are you being distracted by something else? Then remove that distraction. Quit checking your email. Get off Facebook. Just *stop it*. Install software that blocks your access to these websites if you really can't control yourself.

However, on a workcation weekend, it's more likely that your troubles are mental or emotional.

Are you bored? Do you hate your project? If this is the case, ask yourself: are you honestly passionate about this project, or is it more of a should? Is it something you have to do, or can you replace this project with another one?

Have you hit an obstacle? Is it something you can work through on your own, or do you need outside help? If so, can you complete as much of the project as you can on your own, and then save the bits that require assistance for after you return? Or do you need to replace this project with another one?

Mindset problems

Is it too hard? Are you afraid you can't do it? These fears may represent a mindset problem. I talk a lot about mindset in my business mindset books, which is too big of a topic to get into here. Ideally, you'd want to address any fears, blocks, or limiting beliefs you may have about your project *before* you go on your workcation.

If you know you're afraid of your project, see a professional to help you sort out your mindset *before* you go away. If you're stuck with a mindset problem during the workcation, you have a couple of options: you can either sort it out yourself (if you have the skills to do so) or postpone this project and replace it with another one.

If you choose to replace the project, be sure to work with a business mindset coach or another mindset professional (like a PSYCH-K® facilitator or an NLP practitioner) before you attempt to work on this project again.

Can't sleep

I don't usually have trouble falling asleep, but on workcations, I do. My brain often struggles to get out of hyperfocus mode and disconnect from the project I've been working on. There are a few solutions to this.

First, don't eat just before bed, like I used to do on my work-cations. Have an early meal.

The most common piece of advice on how to get to sleep faster involves getting off screens and devices well before bedtime. Blue light from electronic screens can impair our ability to fall asleep. If you're using a computer during your workcation (which you probably will be), then you may be affected by all that screen time.

However, most advice recommends that you avoid electronic devices at least a half-hour before bedtime, meaning that you can improve your chances of falling asleep by getting off your computer at least a half-hour before bed. Listen to a guided meditation or take a relaxing bath. Or go for a nighttime walk.

I also find it helpful to listen to a guided meditation once I'm in bed with the lights out. It helps me to relax and fall asleep. Music like "Weightless" by Marconi Union is perfect for this—it's been called the most relaxing song, and it was designed with relaxation in mind. It's an eight-minute piece, but you can find an extended ten-hour version of it on YouTube, which is probably much longer than you need.

If all else fails, try melatonin (obviously, check with your doctor first, as I am not a health care professional). Melatonin helps me get to sleep right away, so I can get a good night's rest and get up with my alarm when it goes off the next day.

Plan better for next time

Because the workcation involves such a high-intensity type of work, you may need to troubleshoot as you go along. You might notice increased productivity with each getaway. I've certainly tweaked my process and my ritual throughout the last five years of doing monthly workcations.

If your hotel booked you into a street-side room, with noisy traffic that annoyed you, see if it's quieter on the other side of the hotel, perhaps overlooking the car park. Or maybe a higher room would be better. Ask if there's a better option at the same hotel (assuming you liked everything else about it) and then request that when you book in for your next getaway.

If there are no suitable rooms at that hotel, then find somewhere new. Remember what bothered you about the old hotel as you search for a new one, and be sure to avoid those problems on your next workcation.

If your cottage or shepherd's hut was too small and cramped, find a slightly larger place for the next getaway. The tiny shepherd's hut that I went to a couple of times was about the same price as my pretty little cottage (actually, it's more of a summerhouse), and I'm much more comfortable in the larger space. Plus, the view is better.

Do what works for you

If your first workcation isn't a total success, figure out what could make it better, and do that the next time. Don't assume that workcations aren't right for you. Allow yourself to make mistakes, and give it another try.

8

CAN'T I JUST DO IT AT HOME?

"The difference between being an amateur and a pro is that a pro takes the time to create a space to write that honors their creativity."

— MICHELLE KULP

"Can't I just do it at home?" This is an excellent question, and after a year and a half of doing monthly workcations at a hotel, I decided to try one at home. My husband was away, so I thought, "Why spend money on a hotel when I'll be home alone?" I could save money on a cat sitter and test out the idea of doing a workcation at home.

Short story: it didn't work. I tried this a couple of months in a row (because apparently, I'm stubborn), with the same result each time. I ended up changing my selected project for both workcations and choosing to catch up on emails rather than work on one of my books. I managed to get through my emails, but I was disappointed that I hadn't been motivated enough to work on my writing—which was the more critical project.

So stay-at-home workcations most certainly did *not* work for me, but they may work for you, and the only way you'll know is to give it a try. I think they weren't suitable for me because I was trying to focus on my creative projects in my usual workspace. I didn't find a new place, like my garden table or my dining area.

If you're going to attempt a stay-at-home workcation weekend, be sure to find a *new* workspace for your creative project. Don't make the same mistake that I did, and try to do it from your home office or usual work-from-home space. Be a pro. Make it special.

This concept is essential during a global pandemic, where different countries and regions have different restrictions. You may need to switch up your tactic and try a stay-at-home workcation—simply because you're not allowed to leave your home. Don't let a pandemic get in the way of your creative projects. Create the best stay-at-home workcation you can.

When to do it

A stay-at-home workcation is more likely to work during a time when you'll be home alone. Maybe your partner is going on a business trip, and you don't have kids, so you won't have anyone to look after. Or you can make a deal with your partner: they take the kids on a memorable trip to visit their grandparents, perhaps, and you stay at home and work on your project.

Your partner gets time alone with their parents, the kids get to see extended family, and you get time away from them all (while this idea may sound terrible to some, I believe it's healthy for us to spend time away from our partner and family every once in a while).

Workcations are perfect for my own family: my husband and I own a business together, and we both work from home.

We're together all day, every day. We even go on runs together sometimes. We find it healthy to go on our separate workcations so that we each get some alone time.

Where to go

If you do this, be sure to get out of your usual workspace. If you have a home office, then hold your workcation in the dining room. If you have a sunny conservatory, that might work. A summerhouse or garden shed (it's surprising how nice some sheds are!) is also a good choice.

If the weather is clear, and you have a table in the garden, you can work there. We have a tiny round table outside that's really only big enough to have coffee on, but my laptop does fit, and I've done great work out there. I've never had a garden workcation, but I wrote loads of blog posts as I listened to the birdsong from the little blue tit or the cooing of wood pigeons that visited me every day.

Remember: part of the workcation's magic is getting out of your usual workspace and into somewhere new.

What to do

It's still essential for you to follow the basic principles of the workcation weekend: isolate yourself and set boundaries for communication. If you can be home alone, great. If others are there too, make sure that you've put a Do Not Disturb sign on your door—and that people know to respect it.

Be sure to disable notifications on your phone, tablet, and computer. If you have a landline, unplug it and let the calls go to voicemail. Close the tab for your email. Make sure that you are unreachable to the outside world.

Pick *one* project to work on and stick to it. If you know that you won't have an entire weekend to work on your project, but rather a shorter period each day, then adjust your goal accordingly. But don't go into it without a plan.

Create a stay-at-home workcation ritual, and follow it. Your ritual may be different from your workcation away from home, but you should still have a set list of activities that indicate this is a special time to work on a particular project. This is not just any other workday.

Stay focused

Because you'll be at home, you'll have many more distractions than you would in a hotel or a cottage. There will be television, and there may be family. You might have a pile of laundry that you're tempted to pop into the washing machine or dishes that need to be cleaned or put away.

You'll need to ignore all of these distractions, and you'll need to have a steel-strong determination and focus so you can achieve your goals for your stay-at-home workcation. If you suspect you might struggle to stay focused, re-read the previous chapter on How to Stay Focused and make a list of all the things you know will help you get your project completed. Create your own menu of focus-fixes.

Do what works for you

While I am personally skeptical about the feasibility of the stay-at-home workcation weekend, it may work for you. If you can't take a traditional workcation for whatever reason (finances, family, or something else), then by all means do try it at home.

If it doesn't work, then figure out what went wrong, and try again. Keep troubleshooting and tweaking your next workcation. If all else fails, set aside some time and money to have an actual workcation—if not once a month, then once a quarter or once a year. Do what you can.

9

OBJECTIONS

"You miss 100% of the shots you don't take."

— WAYNE GRETZKY

I f you don't try the workcation weekend, then you'll never know the power they have for helping you to get things done. You may be wondering how you'll be able to fit this into your life. You may think you can't do it.

But unless you try, you'll never know. Before you discount the workcation weekend for your life, be sure that your objections are truly unmovable obstacles and not excuses.

Monthly workcation weekends are not for everyone. I'm going to be honest: I don't have children, so I know it's easier for me. But it would also be easy for me to fill up my weekends with other types of activities—courses, workshops, long runs, hiking trips—and yet I continue to make my workcations a priority.

Why? Because they help me to achieve my goals. And my goals are important to me.

No time

You may think that you don't have the time. Is that true? Or could you make the time? If you don't try, you won't know. There are almost always solutions to the "no time" objection.

Even if you're a full-time parent, there are still solutions. Get your partner to watch the kids for a weekend. If you're a single parent, see if you can get a family member or a friend to watch them for a couple of days.

No money

You may think that you don't have the money. Is that true? If that is the case, then see if you can stay somewhere for free. Maybe your parents are going out of town or on holiday, and you can stay at their place for a couple of days. Perhaps your friends have a holiday property that's often empty during the low season. Could they let you have a couple of nights there?

You might also try a website like Housesitters.com. While this may not be ideal (you will be expected to look after the house and any pets), it could be a way to make your workcation happen. It's worth a try.

Remember that this may be a legitimate business expense. Ask your accountant before planning to file this as an expense to be sure. But the way I look at it is this: I could rent a full-time office to use for my workcations, and that would be a tax-deductible expense. But by going on workcation weekends, I'm spending less money than I would for a full-time workspace. So this could save you money on taxes (again, check with your accountant).

Guilt

You may feel guilty about going away by yourself for a couple of days. But would you feel the same if your company sent you on a business trip? This is work. It's just in a different location from where you usually do it.

Other people may try to make you feel guilty. If you're afraid this might happen, then tell no one of your plans. Keep it a secret. No one needs to know but your immediate family (otherwise, your partner might wonder where you've gone).

A male podcaster once interviewed me for his productivity podcast, and we talked all about the workcation weekend. He seemed to think it was a great idea. But do you know what he asked me?

He asked this: "What does your husband think about your monthly workcations?"

I was honestly shocked. While I should have responded, "Would you have asked me that same question if I were a man?" Sadly, I didn't think of that until later. I told the truth: my husband (who is also my business partner) is 100% supportive of my workcations. Why? Because I get things done. I contribute to our publishing business by writing books. My workcation weekends help me to increase our income. My workcations benefit both of us. Yet, even if this is not the case for you, I hope that your partner supports you in being productive and happy.

Your objections

Find out what might be stopping you from booking your first workcation—or your next one, and address that issue. Maybe it's a mindset problem; perhaps it's something else. But get yourself professional help if needed so you can make your workcations a reality.

10

PLAN YOUR OWN WORKCATION

"You don't need a new plan for next year. You need a commitment."

— SETH GODIN

Now it's time for you to plan your first workcation weekend! I'm so excited for you to experience the power of the workcation. This is my number one productivity tool, and I hope it soon becomes yours, too.

Remember: the success of your workcation depends on proper planning. Before diving into it, make sure you get all the elements right. Know what you want and what you don't want. Take time to consider your potential distractions, and plan how you're going to avoid them.

Plan, plan, plan. It doesn't take long, and it will ensure the success of your project.

Before your workcation

1. Select a project or other work to complete.
2. Decide on the best dates for you.
3. Find a hotel or other accommodation and book it.
4. Gather together everything you'll need for your workcation project: print out anything that needs printed, organize all notes, books, etc.
5. Enjoy your workcation!

During your workcation

- Make note of anything that annoys you about your accommodation or location so you can fix it for the next time
- Don't start brainstorming ways to fix the problem for your next location—that's a distraction from the project

After your workcation

- What worked well?
- What didn't work so well?
- Did you experience any distractions? What can you do to avoid them next time?
- Did you have any other problems focusing on your project? What can you do to avoid them next time?
- Will you return to the same location for your next workcation? If not, why not?
- If you need to find a new location, what do you want to avoid in the new place?
- What do you want to ensure the new location has?

For your next workcation

1. Select a new project.
2. Decide on the best dates for you.
3. Book your accommodation.
4. Gather together everything you'll need for your workcation project: print out anything that needs printed, organize all notes, books, etc.
5. Enjoy your workcation!

And so on...

Keep going through this process each time you plan a workcation. Once you've determined that this works for you (and if it doesn't, ask yourself why not), decide how often you want to have a workcation weekend. Quarterly? Monthly? Fortnightly?

Pick a frequency and *get it in your calendar*. Block out the dates, and book your accommodation. I usually only book one workcation at a time, in case I need to change my dates around.

11

GET IN TOUCH

I'd love to hear how it goes! Please send me an email at holly@hollyworton.com and let me know if you have any questions about the workcation process that I haven't covered here.

Everyone I know who has tried a workcation weekend upon my recommendation has had great success. I don't know anyone who continues to do workcations with the regularity that I do, but I also don't know many people who write as much as I do or complete as many projects.

That's not a humblebrag; it's the power of the workcation weekend. I know what works, and I do what it takes to get things done. I have big goals for myself (twelve books in twelve months), and this is how I achieve them.

I hope you find the same success with your workcation weekends.

Good luck!

12

MY WORKCATION PROJECTS

If you'd like to see what types of projects I've created on my workcations, check out my books: https://www.hollyworton.com/books/. Most of them have been written and edited on workcation weekends. I write my shorter books in an entire getaway, and I write my longer books over a series of workcations.

In 2020, I released the second editions of my first five books. These were updated and expanded versions of the original titles, and they were all completed during workcations. While I couldn't go away during lockdown, once restrictions lifted I doubled up and had fortnightly workcations. These helped me to stay on track with my publishing calendar and get things done.

Last year, I hired a coach to help me with my blog. I hadn't been blogging consistently for some time, and I wanted to get back into blogging for SEO. With her help, I crafted a plan for my blog, and I wrote thirty new posts for SEO, many of which were written on workcation weekends. I recently got invited to be on national television, and the producers found me based on one of these blog posts. I'm ranking number one on Google for the exact search term they were looking for. Guess why this great opportunity came to me? It's all thanks to my workcations.

My current website was designed by a professional, but I completed my previous site in a three-day workcation. I did a full re-brand and redesigned all the pages on my own. A friend of mine once doubted my ability to do all this on a single getaway, but then she's never done one herself. She doesn't know the power of the workcation!

APPENDIX I

ON THE PODCAST

The Into the Woods podcast is about personal growth through outdoor adventures—but in a previous incarnation, it was all about business mindset (it used to be called the Business Mindset Podcast.

You can find Holly's show on Apple Podcasts, or wherever you listen to podcasts. Links to subscribe, as well as the full list of episodes, can be found here:

http://www.hollyworton.com/podcast/

The following episodes may be of interest to you. Most of the episodes below have downloadable transcripts (no email required to get the pdf)—or you can read the transcript online in the show notes.

Creativity

- 381 Helen Forester ~ How Getting Outdoors Can Help Us Release Creative Blocks
- 358 Holly Worton ~ How To Write Your Book and Tell Your Story

- 320 Holly Worton ~ Feeling Stuck? Open Up to Receive Creative Downloads Through "Nondoing"
- 304 Holly Worton ~ How To Prioritize When You Can't Do It All
- 298 Jo Casey + Holly ~ What it Takes to Publish Your Book (Both Inner & Outer Work)
- 269 Holly Worton ~ How to Unleash Your Inner Expert
- 265 Holly Worton ~ How to Know if You Should Write a Book For Your Business
- BMP208 Holly Worton ~ What to Do When You Have Nothing to Say
- BMP144 Halona Black ~ How to Create Your Signature Book for Your Business
- R2B126 Sylvie McCracken ~ How to Create Passive Income Through Ebooks
- [SHP 63] How to Self Publish a Book That Looks Professional, with Michele DeFilippo

Mindset

- 333 Holly Worton ~ Do You Have a Fixed Mindset or a Growth Mindset?
- 295 Sharon Lock ~ How to Make Mindset Work a Habit
- 276 Holly Worton ~ How to Create Your Own Personal Formula For Mindset Work & Healing
- 272 Holly Worton ~ Mindset: Why It *Isn't* About Positive Thinking
- 270 Holly Worton ~ Why Mindset Matters
- 245 Holly Worton ~ How to Spring Clean Your Business + Mindset

- 230 Holly Worton ~ How to Make Mindset Work a Habit
- BMP221 Holly Worton ~ How Your Money Mindset Relates to Your Business Mindset
- BMP209 Carmen Spagnola ~ How Nature Can Get You The Right Mindset For Business
- BMP192 Holly Worton ~ Get the Mindset You Need to Make a Big Impact
- BMP181 Jo + Holly ~ Is Mindset Important in Business, or Is It Just an Excuse to Avoid Action?
- BMP170 Denise Duffield-Thomas ~ How Upgrading Your Money Mindset Can Transform Your Business
- BMP157 Holly Worton ~ How to Increase Your Visibility by Transforming Your Mindset
- R2B136 Holly Worton ~ Why You Can't Afford to Ignore Your Business Mindset

Planning

- 379 Holly Worton ~ How to Re-evaluate Your Goals, Plans, and Projects
- 338 Holly Worton ~ How to Achieve Your Goals + Overcome Obstacles, Step By Step

Productivity

- BMP222 Amber De La Garza ~ How to Structure Your Business To Improve Productivity & Get Things Done
- BMP 175 Holly Worton ~ How to Maximize Productivity With a Workcation Weekend

APPENDIX II
PACKING LIST

You may want to adjust this packing list to your needs and save it on your computer so you can use it again and again. You'll be able to print it out when you're packing for your getaway, and you can keep refining the list with each workcation until it's perfect for you.

- Bras + underwear
- Computer glasses
- Cables (Computer, iPhone, iPad)
- Computer + mouse
- Food + snacks
- Glass tea cup (I have a large glass for hot drinks that I bring so I don't have to refill my tea as often)
- Journal (I like to do a gratitude list at the start of each day on the workcation weekend)
- Makeup bag (I sometimes record videos for my YouTube channel in my room, so I like to have makeup with me)
- Melatonin (I often find it difficult to sleep on a workcation weekend because my brain is still raging

with ideas; I take 5mg of melatonin to get to sleep quickly so I can get up early the following morning)

- Notebook + notepad of A4 paper (I have a notebook where I keep written notes for my major projects; the notepad is for making notes as I work on my project)
- Pajamas + hoodie + fluffy socks
- Phone + tablet
- Power talismans (In my case, my fairy wing earrings + fingerless gloves. Bring whatever makes you feel like you're on fire and full of entrepreneurial awesomeness)
- Purse/Backpack
- Scarf (In case the room is chilly in the winter months)
- Sleep mask
- Slippers (I like to take off my shoes as soon as I settle in and put on slippers)
- Socks + Tights
- Sweater/cardigan
- Tea (I like to drink herbal tea nonstop while I work)
- Toiletries
- Video bag (Even if I don't need to do videos, or plan to do videos, I bring my tripod and lapel mic just in case)

BUSINESS BELIEFS

UPGRADE YOUR MINDSET TO OVERCOME SELF-SABOTAGE,
ACHIEVE YOUR GOALS, AND TRANSFORM YOUR BUSINESS
(AND LIFE)

Mindset is an important part of any creative project. For years, I was a business mindset coach, helping entrepreneurs release the fears, blocks, and limiting beliefs that were preventing them from achieving their business goals. While I no longer do this work, I now share my system on how to transform your business mindset in a series of four books.

If you're feeling stuck with your workcation project, you might want to take a look at your subconscious mindset. In these books, you'll learn how to get clear on your current mindset—and the mindset you'll need to achieve your business goals.

The following is an excerpt from my book *Business Beliefs: Upgrade Your Mindset to Overcome Self-Sabotage, Achieve Your Goals, and Transform Your Business (and Life)*. It's available now in ebook, paperback, audiobook, and workbook formats.

~

*"Watch your thoughts, for they become
    words,*
Watch your words, for they become actions,
Watch your actions, for they become habits,
*Watch your habits, for they become your
    character,*
*Watch your character, for it becomes your
    destiny."*

This quote has been misattributed to several people over the years, including Mahatma Gandhi, Ralph Waldo Emerson, Lao Tzu, Gautama Buddha, Bishop Beckwaith, and the father of Margaret Thatcher. The fact that it has been misattributed to so many different people shows just how powerful these words are, and what an impact they've made on a variety of very different cultures. In reality, it doesn't matter who first uttered these words (though if you're curious, according to Quote Investigator (http://quoteinvestigator.com/tag/frank-outlaw/), the earliest evidence of this quote dates from 1977, when it was published in a Texas newspaper that attributed the words to Frank Outlaw, owner of the Bi-Lo supermarket chain).

Never heard of Frank Outlaw? That doesn't matter (although it probably does explain why people have tried to add weight to this quote by misattributing it to more famous people). What matters is that these words are valid: our thoughts and our beliefs create our reality.

Beliefs are the things that we hold to be true, whether or not they are. Beliefs are subjective. They represent an acceptance that someone or something—an idea or a concept—exists or is right, even without proof (for if we had evidence, then this acceptance would be knowledge, rather than belief).

They may also indicate having trust, faith, or confidence in someone or something.

They are the foundation of our personality; they are the elements that we use to define ourselves as individuals. Different people hold different beliefs, and our unique beliefs are part of what makes us who we are. Our ability to step into our greatness and create the business and lifestyle of our dreams depends on our beliefs, which directly influence our behavior.

Beliefs come from every area and every stage of our lives: we form them based on our interactions with authority figures such as our parents, our teachers, our superiors at work. They come from our peers—friends, co-workers, family. We are continually forming beliefs based on our actions and our inter-actions with others. Unfortunately, however, many of our beliefs are not conscious, which is something that we'll examine in the next chapter.

If your mindset is fraught with limiting beliefs, you will struggle to build your business and create the lifestyle you want. On the other hand, if your mindset is supported by beliefs that lift you up, building your dream business will be much, much more manageable. That's why we must keep our beliefs positive and focused on what we *do* want, and not what we *don't* want. Unfortunately, most of us tend to focus on the former.

Watch your thoughts, for they become words

We often express our limiting beliefs in our language. When our current mindset isn't serving us, and a friend asks us how our business is coming along, it can be easy to fall into a victim mentality and say things like:

- "I'm never going to make it. It's just too hard."

- "It's so hard to get clients. I don't know how anyone does it."
- "Building a business is easy for other people. I'm having such a hard time of it myself."

Have you ever heard words like these come out of your mouth? Or maybe you didn't say them. Perhaps they were just thoughts running through your head when you were silently complaining to yourself.

Or maybe you paid too much attention to your mind gremlins, who whispered things like:

- "You're not good enough. You'll never make a living with your business."
- "You're not smart enough to learn all the things you need to learn to market your business."
- "Be careful. If you get too big, people will find out you're a fraud."

Perhaps you found yourself at a business networking meeting, where someone asked you how business was going, and you replied that things were great—yet in the back of your mind, you were thinking just how hopeless you felt. I can't begin to count the times in the early days of my business where people would ask me how things were going, and I would smile and reply enthusiastically. I didn't want to jinx myself by telling the truth, so I pretended everything was fabulous.

Spoiler alert: it wasn't.

These words of self-doubt, whether spoken or unspoken, make up our mindset. Remember: your mindset can support and enhance you and your business, or it can sabotage and undermine you and your business.

Watch your words, for they become actions

Our beliefs are directly related to our actions. If we have confidence in ourselves and if we have a mindset full of firm beliefs about our ability to create a successful business, then we're more likely to take the necessary actions to make that successful business become a reality. On the other hand, if our minds are fraught with limiting beliefs, we're more likely to procrastinate, hiding from the actions that will put us out there, make us visible, and get the clients we need to create our dream business.

A positive mindset will support you in stepping into your greatness. A limiting mindset will keep you stuck in your smallness. Either way, your beliefs influence your actions.

I've seen it so many times with clients: one struggled to create videos for her YouTube channel, which she knew was essential to the growth of her business. She insisted that she wasn't tech-savvy. She spent hours crafting careful scripts, which she would then run through a teleprompter to read as she recorded her videos. This process took hours, and it meant that she put off doing videos as much as possible. After just one session where we focused on changing beliefs around her video creation, she was able to create inspiring, focused videos on YouTube by speaking spontaneously to the camera.

I had another client who also struggled with technology. The more she complained that she didn't know how to do tech things for her online business, the more she remained stuck. We worked on shifting her beliefs around technology, and she was able to work with her web designer to build a new website for her business quickly.

In my own experience, one thing that I've heard myself say more than once is that "I'm not good at play." I often take myself and my business too seriously, forgetting to allow space for fun, play, and joy. And of course, the more I repeat "I'm not good at play," the more truthful that statement becomes. It wasn't until I realized that play could take many forms—some of which I was already practicing—that I understood that I was a playful person and that I could add more play (and therefore more fun!) to my business.

Watch your actions, for they become habits

And, of course, the more you continue to take the same actions, the more they become ingrained. Eventually, they're transformed into habits. You continue to take (or avoid) the same actions, and this only serves to reinforce your neural pathways, keeping you stuck in the same place.

I used to have the bad habit of procrastinating on my emails. I'm talking about messages that I had to respond to personally—emails that I couldn't delegate to an assistant or someone else. I would let them pile up for days in my inbox, and just seeing them would stress me out (though to be fair, having more than twenty emails in my inbox at a time makes me anxious!). I finally started blocking out time in my calendar regularly, where I would force myself to only work on my inbox, and that helped me to get back on track.

Even worse was my track record for returning phone calls. I've since significantly improved in this respect, but for many years I would procrastinate on making phone calls. I'd have them on my list of things to do, but often it would take me *more than a month* to make the calls. I hated phone calls that much. Often, so much time had passed that I would just cross the call off my list because it was no longer relevant.

I used to be extremely organized and tidy. For the most part, I still am, mostly because I get anxious when things are disheveled or out of place. But sometimes, I get into the habit of accumulating a pile of paperwork on my desk—and then not doing anything about it for weeks at a time. Eventually, I'll sift through the papers and process everything, but in the meantime, it looks terrible, and it stresses me out to see it every day. The simple act of adding new papers to that pile soon becomes a habit.

Most unwanted habits can be eliminated by simply changing our behavior. Sometimes that's easy to do, such as in the examples above, but sometimes it's harder. When we notice that we're struggling to shift an unwanted habit, it's time to stop and take a look at our mindset.

What are we afraid of? What are our beliefs about these tasks? I once worked with a client who was behind in doing her tax return. She had boxes and boxes of receipts and paperwork, but she couldn't bear the thought of going through everything. She knew it wouldn't take more than a couple of days to sort through, but she was afraid of what she'd find. And she was scared of how much tax she would owe. Eventually, we did some mindset shifts that made it easier for her to get through the stack of papers, and it was a massive relief. She owed much less than she feared, and she was able to set up more supportive habits for the following tax year.

The easiest way to release these stubborn habits is to change your beliefs. Figure out what you're currently doing that doesn't serve you, and what you'd rather have instead. Then, do the mindset work to make the changes you need to make to have a mindset full of beliefs that support you. You'll learn more about how to do that in later chapters.

Watch your habits, for they become your character

If your habits are made up of the actions that you've taken so many times that they've become almost involuntary, then your character is made up of your unique collection of habits, among other things. The saying goes that actions speak louder than words, and this is especially true in this case. You may think that your mindset is in good shape, but if your actions prove otherwise, then you need to take a look at how your beliefs are influencing your character. I'm sure you've heard the saying: don't pay attention to what people say; pay attention to what they *do*. What do *your* habits say about *you*?

I once knew an entrepreneur who believed himself to be a charismatic and creative leader in his company, but his actions proved him to be an insufferable tyrant. Employee morale was terrible, despite his enthusiastic pep talks. He regularly and consistently micromanaged people (or bullied his managers into doing it for him), and he erupted into tantrums whenever things didn't go his way. These weren't random situations, but consistent and recurring events that eventually showed most people that this was simply the way he was—despite his belief to the contrary.

On the other end of the spectrum, I used to be painfully quiet and shy. This shyness went way back to my school years, where I dreaded being called upon by teachers to answer a question. I would go out of my way to avoid eye contact, even when I knew the answer. I just didn't want to be the center of attention. This quietness continued throughout elementary school into high school, university, and even grad school. I was good at taking tests and writing papers, but I dreaded any kind of verbal participation in class.

The more I avoided it, the worse it got. It wasn't until I joined Toastmasters in 2011—a public speaking club—that not only did I get over my fear of speaking, but I began to enjoy it. It didn't take long before I started to seek out speaking opportunities.

You may believe yourself to be a budding online entrepreneur destined for success, but if you're struggling to send out emails to your list or write a new blog post, you might want to consider what's going on. You can most definitely transform yourself into a successful online business owner, but you're probably going to have to do some work on your beliefs first.

Watch your character, for it becomes your destiny

Destiny often refers to fate or a predetermined and unavoidable course of events. I don't believe in fate or destiny, so for our purposes, let's look at it as the power that determines a sequence of events: let's explore your "destiny" as a successful entrepreneur or business owner. Can you see how your character, which is made up of your thoughts (beliefs), words, actions, and habits, directly influences your ability to create a successful business (or not)?

When you do the mindset work to overcome the fears, blocks, and limiting beliefs that are keeping you stuck, it makes it so much easier to take action—which is what eventually gets you results in your business. At the same time that you release limiting beliefs, it's essential to reprogram your mindset with new beliefs that support you in your business vision. When your business beliefs are aligned with your business goals, action-taking is easy and effortless.

When I used to work with clients, we would dig deep to identify which beliefs were holding them back, and then we changed those beliefs, replacing them with positive, supportive beliefs. We would do work at both the subconscious and energetic levels to create profound, lasting change. At the end of each session, we would create an action plan that involved taking real-life, practical business action toward their goals. When I work with myself, I follow the same process: identify current beliefs, transform them, take action.

In changing your beliefs, you change your destiny. It's that simple.

Take action today

Can you think of examples of how your thoughts—perhaps in the form of mind gremlins—became spoken words that weren't very nice? And can you see how those words influenced your actions, which may have later become habits? Can you see how each of these steps may have affected your character? And finally, can you think of examples of how your words, actions, habits, and character have negatively impacted your business?

On the podcast

You can find the full list of podcast episodes here: www.hollyworton.com/podcast

- 306 Holly Worton ~ How To Create New Habits That Last
- 197 Holly Worton ~ Step into Your Greatness by Upgrading Your Business Beliefs
- 192 Holly Worton ~ Get the Mindset You Need to Make a Big Impact

ABOUT THE AUTHOR

Holly Worton is a podcaster and author. Her 2019 book, *If Trees Could Talk: Life Lessons from the Wisdom of the Woods*, went straight to the top of 16 Amazon bestseller lists, and she has been featured on BBC Radio Scotland and on prime time national television in the UK—on ITV's This Morning and Channel 4's show Steph's Packed Lunch.

She helps people get to know themselves better through connecting with Nature, so they can feel happier and more fulfilled. Holly enjoys spending time outdoors, walking long-distance trails and exploring Britain's sacred sites. She's originally from California and now lives in the Surrey Hills, but has also lived in Spain, Costa Rica, Mexico, Chile, and Argentina. Holly is a member of the Druid order OBOD.

Holly ran her first business for ten years, building it up to become a multi-million-dollar enterprise. When she went into the coaching world she was confident that she had the business and marketing skills she needed to set up a new company. And she did – but she struggled to grow her new venture quickly because she encountered fears, blocks, and limiting beliefs that she didn't even know she had.

Holly discovered that pushing forward and taking action just wasn't enough. She needed to transform her mindset and release her blocks, as this was the only way to take the *right* actions to move her new business forward. Thus began her journey of intense personal development through deep mindset work, which transformed her existing coaching business into a focus on helping people with their business mindset.

Eventually, Holly realized that she wanted to devote her time to helping people through her writing, and she let go of her mindset business to focus on her books. Now, she continues to write about mindset, long-distance walking, and connecting to Nature.

Podcast

You can find her podcast on Apple Podcasts, or wherever you listen to podcasts. Links to subscribe, as well as the full list of episodes, can be found here:

http://www.hollyworton.com/podcast/

Patreon

You can support her work and get access to her ebooks by joining her on Patreon:

https://www.patreon.com/hollyworton

Books

You can find her other work—including her books on business mindset, nature, and walking long-distance trails—wherever you purchased this title.

Newsletter

Finally, you can stay in touch by subscribing to her newsletter on her main website:

http://www.hollyworton.com/

Social media

amazon.com/author/hollyworton

facebook.com/HollyWortonPage

twitter.com/hollyworton

instagram.com/hollyworton

goodreads.com/HollyWorton

bookbub.com/profile/holly-worton

ALSO BY HOLLY E. WORTON

Business Mindset series

- *Business Beliefs: Upgrade Your Mindset to Overcome Self Sabotage, Achieve Your Goals, and Transform Your Business (and Life)*
- *Business Beliefs: A Companion Workbook*
- *Business Blocks: Transform Your Self-Sabotaging Mind Gremlins, Awaken Your Inner Mentor, and Allow Your Business Brilliance to Shine*
- *Business Blocks: A Companion Workbook*
- *Business Visibility: Mindset Shifts to Help You Stop Playing Small, Dimming Your Light and Devaluing Your Magic*
- *Business Visibility: A Companion Workbook*
- *Business Intuition: Tools to Help You Trust Your Own Instincts, Connect with Your Inner Compass, and Easily Make the Right Decisions*
- *Business Intuition: A Companion Workbook*
- *Business Mindset Books: Box Set Books 1-4*

Personal growth

- *The Year You Want*

Into the Woods Short Reads

- *How to Add More Adventure to Your Life*
- *How to Practice Self-Love: Actual Steps You Can Take To*

Love Yourself More
- *How to Practice Self Care: Even When You Think You're Too Busy*
- *How to Develop Your Own Inner Compass: Learn to Trust Yourself and Easily Make the Best Decisions*
- *Into the Woods Short Reads: Box Set Books 1-5*

Nature books

- *If Trees Could Talk: Life Lessons from the Wisdom of the Woods*
- *If Trees Could Talk: Life Lessons from the Wisdom of the Woods — A Companion Workbook*

Walking books

- *Alone on the South Downs Way: A Tale of Two Journeys from Winchester to Eastbourne*
- *Walking the Downs Link: Planning Guide & Reflections on Walking from St. Martha's Hill to Shoreham-by-Sea*
- *Alone on the Ridgeway: A Tale of Two Journeys Between Avebury and Ivinghoe Beacon*
- *Walking the Wey-South Path: Planning Guide & Reflections on Walking from Guildford to Amberley*

En español

- *Si los árboles hablaran: enseñanzas de vida desde la sabiduría de los árboles*
- *El año que quieres: imagina la vida que deseas y planea tu año ideal, para no dejarlos al azar*

REVIEW TEAM

Would you like to be a part of my review team?

I really value the feedback and reviews I get from my readers. They make a huge difference in helping me (and other authors) reach new people. I know that it takes time to read and review a book, and I value the time people put into this. Thank you so much!

Here's what's involved....

Advance Review Copies

Whenever I have a new book coming out, I will send you an email to see if you would like to get an advance ebook copy for review on Amazon and/or Goodreads (or elsewhere online!).

If you are able to write an honest review by the deadline (I'll let you know about the timeline), then I'll send over a copy for you to read before it's on sale to the general public.

I can also send you free copies of any of my existing books (ebooks or audio) if you'd like to review them.

Audiobooks

If you enjoy audiobooks, I can also provide free audiobook codes so you can listen to the new audiobooks and review online. I don't produce all of my books as audiobooks, but I will offer you codes for the ones that are available.

Your review

If you enjoy the book, please post your review on Amazon.com or your local Amazon.

You can also post reviews on the online bookstores, social media, your blog, and anywhere else you feel like sharing. Amazon is the biggie for online reviews, but Goodreads, Instagram, and other online outlets all help.

Unsubscribe

This is a simple email list, so if you change your mind about being involved for whatever reason, you can unsubscribe from the list at any time.

Join now

If you would like to join, please fill out the form on my website and then look out for an email confirmation. Learn more here: https://www.hollyworton.com/review-team/.

HOLLY'S GROVE

I'd love for you to join me in my private community for readers, Patrons, clients, and students only. It's a place to talk about tree communication and outdoors adventures—and creative work like the types of projects you can complete on a workcation.

If you have any questions about how to improve your own workcations, you can ask them in there.

I'll also be sharing updates about my upcoming book projects and launches.

I'd love to get to know you in there!

You can find it here:
http://hollyworton.com/grove

A REQUEST

If you enjoyed this book, please review it online. It takes just a couple of minutes to write a quick review. It would mean the world to me! Good reviews help other readers to discover new books.

Thank you, thank you, thank you.